WE THE PEOPLE

The Hindenburg

by Marc Tyler Nobleman

Content Adviser: Knox Bishop,
Former Curator, Frontiers of Flight Museum,
Dallas, Texas

Reading Adviser: Rosemary G. Palmer, Ph.D.,
Department of Literacy, College of Education,
Boise State University

COMPASS POINT BOOKS
MINNEAPOLIS, MINNESOTA

Compass Point Books
3109 West 50th Street, #115
Minneapolis, MN 55410

Visit Compass Point Books on the Internet at *www.compasspointbooks.com*
or e-mail your request to *custserv@compasspointbooks.com*

On the cover: The Hindenburg exploding at Lakehurst, New Jersey, on May 6, 1937.

Photographs ©: Sam Shere/Getty Images, cover, 27; Prints Old and Rare, back cover (far left);
Library of Congress, back cover, 20; Fox Photos/Getty Images, 4; Bettmann/Corbis, 6, 26, 31, 32,
41; Corbis, 7, 16, 17, 18, 36; Hulton Archive/Getty Images, 8, 29; Mary Evans Picture Library,
10, 21; Central Press/Getty Images, 12; General Photographic Agency/Getty Images, 13, 19;
New York Times Co./Getty Images, 14, 24, 39; Hirz/Getty Images, 23; Bob Gomel/Time Life
Pictures/Getty Images, 25; Arthur Cofod/Pictures Inc./Time Life Pictures/Getty Images, 28;
Time Life Pictures/Mansell/Getty Images, 30, 40; The Granger Collection, New York, 35;
Jack Benton/Hulton Archive/Getty Images, 37.

Managing Editor: Catherine Neitge
Designer/Page Production: Bradfordesign, Inc./Bobbie Nuytten
Photo Researcher: Marcie C. Spence
Cartographer: XNR Productions, Inc.
Educational Consultant: Diane Smolinski
Library Consultant: Kathleen Baxter

Creative Director: Keith Griffin
Editorial Director: Carol Jones

Library of Congress Cataloging-in-Publication Data
Nobleman, Marc Tyler.
  The Hindenburg / by Marc Tyler Nobleman.
      p. cm.—(We the people)
  Includes bibliographical references and index.
  ISBN 0-7565-1266-2 (hardcover)
  1. Hindenburg (Airship)—Juvenile literature. 2. Aircraft accidents—New Jersey—Juvenile
literature. I. Title. II. We the people (Series) (Compass Point Books)
  TL659.H5.N63 2005
  363.12'465—dc22   2005002464

TABLE OF CONTENTS

DANGEROUS CROSSING

Fourteen-year-old Werner Franz had a great job. The German teenager was a "mess boy" aboard the *Hindenburg*, the largest airship that had ever flown. The *Hindenburg* was a dirigible—a lighter-than-air, engine-powered craft. It resembled a massive cucumber-shaped

The massive dirigible Hindenburg

balloon, but it didn't drift along with the prevailing winds like a balloon—it was steered. The huge dirigible stretched as long as three football fields. Beginning in 1936, it carried passengers back and forth between Germany and North and South America.

Werner helped the adult crew with various tasks. Riding the *Hindenburg* was thrilling, but sometimes dangerous. At times, he had to climb up or down ladders and across catwalks inside the ship to deliver things from one crew member to another.

In 1937, Werner discovered that just being on the *Hindenburg* was more dangerous than crossing the catwalks inside it. As the dirigible was coming in for a landing over a New Jersey airfield, something rocked it. The dinner plates Werner was cleaning at that moment crashed to the floor and broke. He did not know it yet, but the rear section of the airship had burst into flames.

In seconds, the majestic *Hindenburg* was raging with fire. As the ship crashed to the earth, Werner prayed.

The Hindenburg, *several seconds after it burst into flames*

Then he kicked open a service hatch, jumped out of the collapsing dirigible, and was doused with water, which saved him from the fire. He sprinted away from the wreckage, and although shaken up, Werner Franz was otherwise unhurt.

However, 36 others did not have Werner's luck.

DAWN OF THE DIRIGIBLE

Before airplanes could offer long-distance passenger flights, there were dirigibles. Travelers who could afford it crossed the Atlantic Ocean in these enormous, graceful airships. From the outside, dirigibles looked like science fiction come to life. On the inside, they looked like hotels.

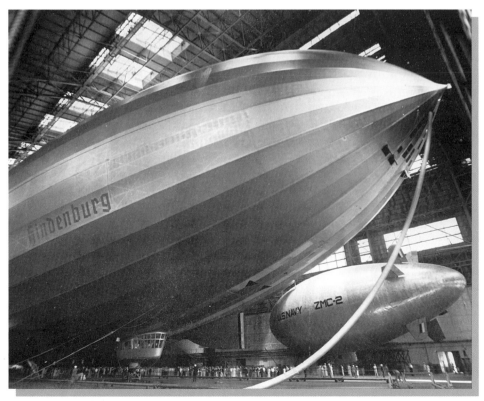

The huge Hindenburg *had only inches to spare when parked in a hangar.*

7

Some dirigibles held their shape only from the pressure of the lifting gas inside. These nonrigid airships are called blimps. Others, including the *Hindenburg*, were rigid airships supported by an internal metal skeleton that held 16 gas bags. Although differing in size, both nonrigid and rigid airships were covered by a colossal outer skin called the envelope.

In 1900, a German named Count Ferdinand von Zeppelin launched the first successful rigid airship. It stayed aloft for 18 minutes. He founded a company he called Zeppelin.

Zeppelin's airline flew more than 14,000 passengers on

Ferdinand von Zeppelin (right), with engineer Hugh Eckener, who would continue Zeppelin's work

sightseeing trips across Germany starting in 1909. During World War I (1914–1918), the Germans flew dirigibles for military action, dropping bombs from them on London, England, and other cities in Europe. The dirigibles were also used as long-range scouts for the German navy.

After the war, the dirigible had a different purpose. It became the world's first transatlantic passenger airliner. Airplanes existed already, but they were more limited in the amount of weight they could carry. They also could not travel long distances without landing to refuel. Dirigible airships did not have these limitations. At the time, people thought dirigibles would become the primary method of traveling long distances.

Yet the glory days of dirigibles as passenger airlines did not last long. One of the few dirigibles used for passenger transportation was the *Hindenburg*. It was supposed to be the first of a fleet. Its tragic end in 1937 made it the last dirigible passenger airliner.

Paul von Hindenburg was president of Germany from 1925 to 1934.

FEATURES AND FLAWS

The destruction of the *Hindenburg* made it legendary, but it was a remarkable technological invention before that. It took five years to build, from 1931 to 1936, and was named for the former president of Germany, Paul von Hindenburg, who died in 1934. At 804 feet (245 meters) long and 135 feet (41 m) in diameter at its widest point, the *Hindenburg* was a true giant of the sky, more than three times bigger than the commercial jets of today. The airship was powered by four 16-cylinder diesel engines, two on each side. Its gas was stored in 16 large cells.

German engineers originally planned to fill the *Hindenburg* with helium, a gas that does not burn. At the time, the United States was the world's only commercial source of large amounts of helium. The U.S. government worried that German dictator Adolf Hitler and his Nazi government would use helium to make

11

military airships, so the United States refused to sell any to Germany. The Germans had to redesign their airship so it could lift with hydrogen, a flammable gas.

In doing so, they had to create more safety measures to minimize the risk of fire. They coated the fabric of the airship's outer covering with a chemical substance that would reflect sunlight and keep the hydrogen inside from overheating. This coating was also waterproof. But one of the ingredients in the coating was aluminum powder, which burns easily.

The passenger decks of some dirigibles were inside a boxlike section

12

The Hindenburg *under construction in Friedrichshafen, Germany*

attached to the bottom of the envelope. The passenger decks of the *Hindenburg* were at the bottom as well—but built within the body of the envelope, not hanging down. This made the *Hindenburg* more aerodynamic.

The Hindenburg's *coating reflected sunlight and was waterproof.*

PALACE IN THE CLOUDS

Like the ill-fated *Titanic* before it, the *Hindenburg* was considered the peak of elegance in its day. Both built to carry passengers across the Atlantic Ocean, the *Titanic* floated on water and the *Hindenburg* floated on air. The

The crew had to strain to control the mooring ropes of the Hindenburg *when it landed.*

Hindenburg was only 78 feet (23.7 m) shorter than the *Titanic*, which sank on its maiden voyage in 1912.

Flying on the *Hindenburg* was expensive. A one-way ticket cost $400 (about the same price as a new car at that time), and a round-trip ticket cost $720. Though people were paying for extravagance, they were also paying for speed since the *Hindenburg* was faster than a steamship. The *Hindenburg's* top speed was 82 miles (131 km) per hour. An average crossing from Europe west to the United States took about two and a half days (64 ½ hours), while an eastbound trip took about two days (52 hours). A trip on most ocean liners took about six days.

The two promenades of the *Hindenburg* offered a dazzling view of the scenery below through rows of large windows, which could be opened. This was possible because the standard cruising altitude was 650 feet (198 m), much lower than airplanes. A baby grand piano (made mostly of aluminum and covered in yellow pigskin) and a mural of famous explorers adorned the lounge.

The dining hall was next to a promenade where passengers could look out.

The dining hall served food of the highest quality. The airship had a reading and writing room stocked with *Hindenburg* stationery. Modern conveniences included electric lights and telephones.

The *Hindenburg* also had a smoking room where people were allowed to smoke a cigarette, cigar, or pipe. This was an astounding allowance for a ship that was filled with flammable gas. The room was pressurized so

Passengers napped and relaxed in the Hindenburg's *lounge.*

no hydrogen could leak in, and people entered and left it
through an air lock door. Since all passengers' matches and
lighters were collected by the crew upon boarding, the
smoking room had the only available electric lighter on the
ship. It was attached with a cord so it could not be removed.

Passenger cabins were 5 feet by 6 ¼ feet (1.5 m by 2 m). That was small, but passengers did not spend much time in their rooms anyway. Cabins contained two berths, bunk bed style, plus a fold-up sink and a collapsible writing table. Travelers shared several toilets and a single shower.

Passenger cabins on the Hindenburg *were quite plain.*

DESTINATION LAKEHURST

The *Hindenburg* first took to the skies in March 1936 for several test flights. Later that month, with the Nazi swastika symbol painted on its tail fins, it began a propaganda tour. The airship blasted patriotic music from loudspeakers as it dropped leaflets and small flags promoting the Nazi party on German towns. After the tour, passenger service kicked off.

The Hindenburg *had giant Nazi swastika symbols painted on it.*

The USS Los Angeles *enters the hangar at Lakehurst Naval Air Station in 1924.*

Not every airfield could handle a dirigible launch and landing. Dirigibles required a huge hangar and many people on the ground. Approximately 200 crew members were needed to guide a dirigible to and from a hangar with mooring lines. The U.S. government agreed to let the *Hindenburg* land at the Lakehurst Naval Air Station in Lakehurst, New Jersey. It had been the home of the lighter-than-air operations for the U.S. Navy since 1921.

On May 6, 1936, the *Hindenburg* departed on its first transatlantic voyage, taking passengers from Germany to the United States. Before the end of 1936, it made nine more round trips on that route. In between that busy schedule, it was put on display at the opening ceremonies of the 1936 Olympics in Berlin.

On May 3, 1937, the *Hindenburg* prepared to take off from Frankfurt, Germany, headed for Lakehurst. As was traditional, Captain Max Pruss shouted *"Schiff hoch!"* which means "Up ship!" The ground crew released the mooring lines. The *Hindenburg* rose straight up into the air, and so began its 21st transatlantic flight.

The *Hindenburg* could hold 72 passengers, but on this trip it carried exactly half. The return trip, which never took place, was fully booked. Most would-be passengers planned to attend the coronation of England's King George VI.

The 36 passengers on the *Hindenburg* included American

In between transatlantic trips, the Hindenburg *flew over the opening ceremonies of the 1936 Olympics.*

21

and German businesspeople, writers, soldiers, and even an acrobat. The youngest passengers were 6- and 8-year-old brothers traveling with their parents and older sister. Sixty-one crew members were also onboard, 20 more than usual since some were in training. No one knew they were on the *Hindenburg's* final voyage.

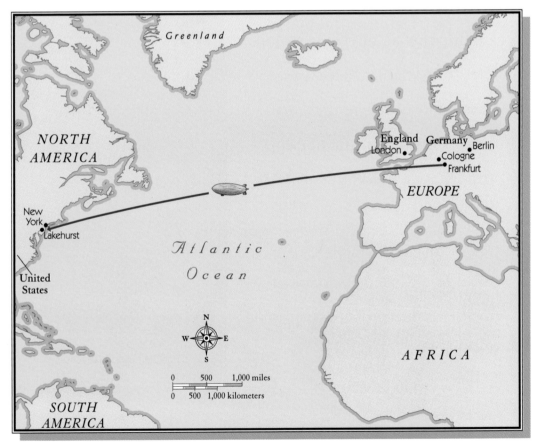

The Hindenburg's *final trip was the first of the 1937 travel season.*

PANIC IN THE SKY

Flying on the *Hindenburg* was smooth. Some people onboard were so relaxed that they did not realize when the airship had taken off. During the trip, they sang at the piano, wrote postcards, listened to the news, which was broadcast into the lounge, and gazed out the windows at Earth passing underneath.

On May 6, three days after leaving Germany, the *Hindenburg* reached the United States. That date was the anniversary of its first departure for a transatlantic flight. Reporters, along with family and friends of the passengers,

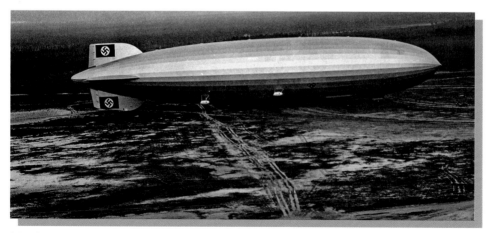

The lighter-than-air Hindenburg

23

waited at Lakehurst. Many of them had been there since early morning. The dirigible had been expected at 6 A.M. but did not arrive until afternoon because of the weather. Thunder rumbled and rain fell throughout the day.

Regulations prevented Captain Pruss from landing during such unfavorable weather. Wind and lightning could pose a major problem for lighter-than-air ships during landing. To wait out the stormy conditions, he took the passengers on an aerial tour of New York City. They had a magnificent view of the Statue of Liberty, Empire State Building, Times Square, Central Park, and Ebbets Field, where the Brooklyn Dodgers were playing a baseball game with the Pittsburgh Pirates.

The Hindenburg *flew over the skyscrapers of lower Manhattan and the Brooklyn Bridge.*

24

The *Hindenburg* passed
Lakehurst, New Jersey, around
4 P.M. But the weather was not
clear enough to attempt
landing. Captain Pruss con-
tinued to stall, flying over
the New Jersey shore. At
6 P.M., the rain became heavy
for about 10 minutes, then
tapered to a drizzle. At
6:12 P.M., Commander Charles
E. Rosendahl, the commanding

Charles E. Rosendahl discussed the
Hindenburg *crash in later years.*

officer at Lakehurst, sent a message to Pruss: "Conditions
now considered suitable for landing." Pruss directed the
airship to return to the airfield. At 6:23 P.M., Rosendahl
sent a more urgent message: "Recommend landing now."

By 7 P.M., the *Hindenburg* approached Lakehurst
again. The dirigible maneuvered around the airfield at an
altitude of 650 feet (198 m). It hovered as crew members in

The Hindenburg, *seconds before bursting into flames*

the airship and on the ground prepared for landing. It was going to dock at a tall pole called a mooring mast. When the airship was less than 300 feet (91.5 m) high, the crew began to guide it using the mooring lines.

At 7:25 P.M., at a height of 260 feet (79 m), something went wrong. People on the ground heard a noise and saw a small, mushroom-shaped lick of fire shoot up from the top of the *Hindenburg*, just in front of the rear fin. The noise was not loud. Various witnesses compared it to a beer bottle being opened, a gas stove being turned on, or a rifle being fired. Some say the flame was preceded by a blue glow. Others noticed a pink glow from within the ship.

Though this initial sign of trouble seemed different to different people, the next sign appeared the same to all. The tail of the *Hindenburg* exploded into flames.

The Hindenburg *explodes as it nears the mooring mast.*

27

ONLY SECONDS TO REACT

The blaze roared rapidly toward the front of the *Hindenburg*, consuming half of the hull in seconds. For a moment, the dirigible stayed level. Then the rear of the ship began plummeting toward the ground, tipping the nose toward the heavens. Flames erupted from the middle of the ship, and more flames blew out through the nose. Inside, terrified passengers and crew were tossed about. Below, spectators scrambled to get out of its way.

The pressure wave of the explosion widened out in a circle away from the Hindenburg.

Desperate to escape, passengers and crew members jumped from windows and slid down ropes as horrified onlookers watched. Some did not survive the fall. One man considered using bed linens to cushion his fall, but the ship touched down before he could get them. He and his wife leapt from the charred framework anyway, and lived.

A victim is carried away from the wreckage of the Hindenburg.

The middle of the *Hindenburg* was engulfed in fire before the tail slammed into the ground. The rest of the fiery airship sank with a thick clump of smoke billowing from it. The outer covering had burned away, revealing the skeleton underneath, black and battered in the inferno. Firefighters raced to the scene to douse the fire.

The *Hindenburg* was gone. From normal operation to utter destruction, only 34 seconds had passed.

Flames consume the Hindenburg.

THE HUMANITY

The *Hindenburg* catastrophe was captured live by a Chicago radio reporter named Herbert Morrison. His emotional account was recorded as the event was happening. A shocked nation heard it on the radio the next day. In later documentaries, his grief-stricken words accompanied film footage of the accident, but he was recording sound only, not visuals.

Crouching low on the ground, spectators who had come to watch the Hindenburg *land, instead saw it burst into flames.*

31

Morrison was at Lakehurst awaiting the *Hindenburg's* arrival with the rest of the crowd. As he watched the dirigible disintegrate, he shouted what sounds like "Oh, the humanity!" This has become the most widely repeated exclamation associated with the *Hindenburg* disaster.

Here is a portion of what Morrison said. Charlie was his sound engineer.

News photographers were expecting a routine landing when disaster struck the Hindenburg *at Lakehurst.*

It's burst into flames! Get out of the way! Get out of the way! Get this, Charlie! Get this, Charlie! It's fire and it's crashing! It's crashing terrible! Oh, my! Get out of the way, please! It's burning, bursting into flames and is falling on the mooring mast, and all the folks between. This is terrible. This is the worst of the worst catastrophes in the world! Oh, it's crashing ... oh, four or five hundred feet into the sky, and it's a terrific crash, ladies and gentlemen. There's smoke, and there's flames, now, and the frame is crashing to the ground, not quite to the mooring mast. Oh, the humanity, and all the passengers screaming around here!

I told you ... I can't even talk to people ... around there. It's—I can't talk, ladies and gentlemen. Honest, it's just laying there, a mass of smoking wreckage, and everybody can hardly breathe and talk. ... I, I'm sorry. Honest, I can hardly breathe. I'm going to step inside where I cannot see it. Charlie, that's terrible. I—listen folks, I'm going to have to stop for a minute, because I've lost my voice. This is the worst thing I've ever witnessed.

MORE LIVED THAN DIED

Although spectators feared that no one inside the *Hindenburg* survived, more people lived than died. Of the 97 people onboard, 62 survived. Thirteen passengers and 22 crew members perished. One man on the ground was also killed, bringing the total death toll to 36. Captain Pruss was one of the survivors. He was badly burned and lingered near death for days, but eventually recovered. The *Hindenburg's* former captain, Ernst Lehman, was onboard as an observer. He was badly burned and died the next day.

Immediately, people began to search for the cause of the fire. Hitler called it an "act of God." To this day, no definitive reason has been determined, but there are several theories.

Some think that an electrical spark started the fire. Though such a spark could have been caused by lightning, it was unlikely because the *Hindenburg* had previously

The front page of the May 7 San Francisco Chronicle; the actual death toll was 36

flown through lightning storms without being damaged. A spark also could have been caused by static. Because of the rain, the airship and its mooring lines were wet. When the mooring lines were dropped, they connected the metal frame of the ship to the ground, which could have caused an electrical discharge.

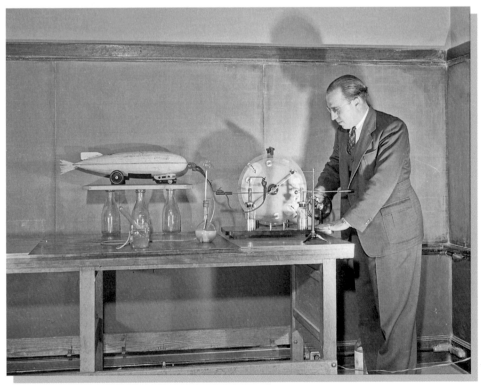

Michael Fiore believed static electricity caused the disaster and set up a demonstration on May 10, 1937, to prove his point.

Some believe the *Hindenburg* was sabotaged. Since the crash happened as World War II loomed in Europe, this theory was popular at the time, especially among the crew. The ship was the pride of Adolf Hitler, so some people think an anti-Nazi passenger planted a bomb onboard. The U.S. Federal Bureau of Investigation had suspects, but did not find firm evidence.

What ignited the fire is one mystery. What enabled it to burn so quickly is another. The Germans who built the *Hindenburg* knew their safety precautions were not foolproof.

Sailors and military officers stand near the Hindenburg *the day after it crashed.*

37

The fire spread because of the hydrogen gas in the envelope or the coating applied to the envelope fabric. Both were flammable.

Some think that hydrogen was to blame, while others think it was the coating. Those who defend the fabric point out that once the fire started, everything burned, not just the fabric.

Those who defend the hydrogen say that hydrogen burns invisibly, yet the *Hindenburg's* flames were visible. In addition, hydrogen burns upward, but the *Hindenburg's* flames burned downward. Also, since hydrogen is a colorless, odorless gas, the scent of garlic had been added to it so people onboard would be able to detect a leak. Nobody reported smelling garlic that day. The gauges on the ship did not show a leak either.

A different theory is that mechanical failure caused a gas leak that ignited. Yet another theory is that someone on the ground shot the ship down. The truth may never be known.

Joachim Breithaupt (left) of Germany and Commander Charles E. Rosendahl of Lakehurst Naval Air Station lay wreaths at the charred remains of the Hindenburg.

When the *Hindenburg* crashed in 1937, people had been flying dirigibles for nearly three decades. Though the *Hindenburg* was not the first to crash, it was the most devastating. After the public watched newsreel footage of the disaster and heard the chilling radio broadcast, many no

The burning wreckage of the Hindenburg

longer trusted dirigibles. By 1939, commercial airplane service began and would replace commercial dirigible service entirely.

By going down in flames, the *Hindenburg* went down in history. For a year, it symbolized grandness. For a day, it embodied tragedy. Despite its ultimate failure, the last of the long-distance passenger dirigibles had many admirers. They imagined how peaceful it must have been to soar across the ocean in something so large and yet lighter than air.

Many chose to remember the Hindenburg *in her glory, not her destruction.*

41

GLOSSARY

aerodynamic—designed to move through the air easily

air lock—an enclosure between two airtight doors to permit passage from one space to the other

catwalks—narrow walkways high in the air

hull—the frame or body of a ship or aircraft

inferno—an intense fire

mess boy—a boy helper aboard a ship

mooring line—a device that holds a ship or aircraft securely in place

Nazi—a member of the National Socialist Party led by Adolf Hitler that controlled Germany before and during World War II (1939–1945); the Nazi emblem was the swastika, an ancient religious symbol

promenades—decks on a ship where passengers can stroll

propaganda—information spread to try to influence the thinking of people; often not completely true or fair

sabotaged—to have damaged, destroyed, or interfered with on purpose

42

DID YOU KNOW?

- Olympic rings were painted on the side of the *Hindenburg* for its appearance at the 1936 summer Olympics in Berlin.

- Before heading for the United States on what would be its final flight, the *Hindenburg* dropped a bag of mail over the German city of Cologne.

- The *Hindenburg* was four times larger than the Goodyear blimp.

- Two dogs onboard the *Hindenburg* died when it crashed.

- Hugo Eckener, president of the Zeppelin company, deeply resented the Nazis' use of the *Hindenburg* for propaganda purposes. Because of Eckener's many public comments, the Nazis declared him a "nonperson" in Germany's newspapers. As the Nazis gained power, Eckener lost his job.

Important Dates

Timeline

1900	A rigid airship flies for the first time, staying in the air for 18 minutes.
1909	Zeppelin launches airship sightseeing trips across Germany.
1914	Dirigibles flown for military action during World War I.
1931	Construction begins on the Hindenburg dirigible.
1936	The Hindenburg is completed and makes its maiden voyage from Germany to the United States in May.
1937	The Hindenburg burns and crashes on May 6 while attempting to land in New Jersey, killing 36 people and marking the end of commercial dirigible travel.

IMPORTANT PEOPLE

WERNER FRANZ (1922–)

German mess boy who survived the Hindenburg *crash and, in 2004 at age 82, came from Germany to Lakehurst to attend a dedication ceremony of the Navy Lakehurst Information Center*

ADOLF HITLER (1889–1945)

German dictator from 1933 to 1945, during which time the Hindenburg *first flew and was later destroyed*

HERBERT MORRISON (1905–1989)

Correspondent for Chicago radio station WLS whose live audio coverage of the Hindenburg *disaster is widely known*

MAX PRUSS (1891–1960)

Captain of the Hindenburg *on its final flight*

CHARLES E. ROSENDAHL (1892–1977)

Commanding officer at Lakehurst Naval Air Station on the day the Hindenburg *crashed*

FERDINAND VON ZEPPELIN (1838–1917)

German businessman credited with creating the first successful rigid airship and the company that would bear his name to produce airships

45

WANT TO KNOW MORE?

At the Library

Archbold, Rick. *The Hindenburg: An Illustrated History.* New York:
Warner Books, 1994.

De Angelis, Gina. *The Hindenburg.* Philadelphia: Chelsea House
Publications, 2000.

Deady, Kathleen W. *The Hindenburg: Fiery Crash of a German Airship.*
Mankato, Minn.: Capstone Press, 2002.

Majoor, Mireille, and Ken Marschall. *Inside the Hindenburg.* New York:
Little Brown and Company, 2000.

O'Brien, Patrick. *The Hindenburg.* New York: Henry Holt & Company, 2000.

On the Web

For more information on the *Hindenburg*, use FactHound
to track down Web sites related to this book.

1. Go to *www.facthound.com*

2. Type in a search word related to this book
   or this book ID: 0756512662

3. Click on the *Fetch It* button.

Your trusty FactHound will fetch the best Web sites for you!

On the Road

Frontiers of Flight Museum

6911 Lemmon Ave.

Love Field

Dallas, Texas

214/350-3600

To view the aviation museum's

Lighter than Air display on airships

The Hindenburg Memorial

Naval Air Engineering Station

Lakehurst, New Jersey

732/244-8861

To learn about the Navy Lakehurst

Historical Society's memorial service

on May 6 of each year at 7:25 P.M. to

commemorate those killed in the

Hindenburg disaster and other

airship crashes

Look for more We the People books about this era:

Angel Island

The Great Chicago Fire

Great Women of the

   Suffrage Movement

The Harlem Renaissance

The Haymarket Square Tragedy

Industrial America

The Johnstown Flood

The Lowell Mill Girls

Roosevelt's Rough Riders

A complete list of We the People titles is available on our Web site:
www.compasspointbooks.com

INDEX

About the Author

Marc Tyler Nobleman is the author of more than 40 books for young people. He writes regularly for *Nickelodeon Magazine* and has written for The History Channel. He is also a cartoonist whose single panels have appeared in more than 100 international publications, including the *Wall Street Journal, Good Housekeeping,* and *Forbes.* He lives with his wife and daughter in Connecticut.